KILL COLD CALLS

STEVE JOLLY

Steve Jolly Publishing
Nashville, TN

Copyright © 2017 Steve Jolly. All Rights Reserved.

Published by Steve Jolly, Nashville TN

No part of this book may be reproduced, stored, or transmitted in any form and by any means without the prior written permission of the publisher. Requests to the publisher should be sent to Steve Jolly at stevejolly@nashvillerealestatenow.com.

Limits of Liability/Disclaimer of Warranty: While the author and publisher have used their best efforts in preparing this book, they make no warranties or representations with respect to the accuracy or completeness of this book. No warranty may be created or extended. The advice and strategies within might not be suitable for your use or situation. The author and/or publisher do not guarantee that anyone following these techniques, suggestions, tips, ideas, or strategies will become successful. The author and/or publisher shall have neither liability nor responsibility to anyone with respect to any loss or damage caused, or alleged to be caused, directly or indirectly, by the information contained in this book.

Consult with a professional where appropriate. Neither the publisher nor the author shall be liable for damages arising herefrom.

All trademarks and service marks are the properties of their owners. All references to these are made solely for editorial purposes. Except for those owned by the author or publisher, no commercial claims are made to their use. Neither the author nor publisher is associated with these marks in any way.

How to generate a six-figure real estate income like direct marketing legends without cold calls.

Foreword

The Secret to Our Success

I fully believe the secret to our success in business is how we treat people. We carry this attitude into everything we do. You might think it sounds trite or that it couldn't be that easy. The truth is, such kindness is not easy. If it were easy, everyone would be doing it.

This goes beyond "world class service" and "treating them as friends."

To a level that I call, "treating them like family." I don't mean the kind of family like your crazy, old uncle. It's treating people like you would a member of your immediate family.

This is what we all want, but rarely get.

This kind of service blows people away and has them singing your praises at the top of the mountain. This is what can cause the exponential growth in your referral business.

So anytime you are in contact with a customer or client, keep that in mind.

When you treat people like family, they tend to treat you the same.

Table of Contents

Foreword i
    The Secret to Our Success i

Table of Contents iii

Introduction 1
    It started with a simple email and a commitment to keep writing 2
    Why email is the best place to start with content marketing? .. 2
    The Filter Factor 5
    Email = Leverage 6
    2012 Obama Email Campaign 7
    Recent Studies 8
    Why Not Text? 8
    Keep it Simple 9
    Tips and Tricks 9
    Ready to Start? 10

1 Know Your Audience and Market 13
    Start With Your Audience 14
    Researching your audience 15
    Market Research Questions to Ask and Find Answers 16
    The Customer Persona 17
    Write with Authenticity 19
    Know, Like, and Trust 20
    Discovering the Real You 21
    Conversion Theory 22

    Online Conversion Pathway 23

2 How to Add Value **27**
    Story Themes That Add Value 30

3 The Email Pattern **35**
    Headline 37
    Opening 37
    Story 38
    Sell 39
    Close 40
    Tips and Tricks 40

4 Headlines **43**
    The Theme 46
    Headline Analysis 47
    Headline Examples by Theme 48
    Examples of Real-Life Boring Headlines 50
    Headline Inspiration 50
    Tips and Tricks 51

5 The Opening **53**
    Examples of Story Openings by Theme 54
    Other Common Opening Themes for Stories 56
    Study the Openings of Other Stories 57
    Tips and Tricks 57

6 The Story **59**
    Types Of Stories That Influence and Build Trust 60
    Tips and Tricks 66

7 The Sell **67**
    The Segue 68
    The Call to Action [CTA] 70
    Consistency in Action 73
    Multiple CTAs 74
    Examples of The Sell 75
    Tips and Tricks 75

8 The Closing 77
Second CTA 78
Other Options for the Close 79
The Footer Needs Love Too 80
Tips and Tricks 80

9 How to Convert Online Leads 83
Tools 84
Systems 88
How to add automation to this system 95

10 Real Email Examples 101
Inspirational 101
Origin Stories 103
Shocking 105
Demonstation 107
Pop Culture 108
Current Events 110
Conflicting Information 112
Taking a Stand 113
Social Proof 115
Answering Questions 118

Introduction

"I bet phone calls piss you off."

~ Gary Vaynerchuk - Best Selling Author, Speaker & Owner of VaynerMedia

You hate cold calling.

And you are not the only one.

We all know that you can do it. But, it's damaging to your psyche because you were not made for it. You don't want to take the calls, let alone make them.

It takes a special person to be able to be bothersome for a living.

It's more than annoying people all day that turned me off of cold calling. (And I used it successfully in three different industries.)

That's not the way most successful businesses are created and grown today. Cold calls have gotten so out of favor with the public, that they are inefficient.

Time is the most precious commodity that you have, so you should never waste it. Especially when there is a better way.

Finally, cold calling makes people quit sales. Even the best will eventually hate their job if they are not wired to dial all day.

That's why I set out an a mission to find a better way to build relationships that lead to sales.

It started with a simple email and a commitment to keep writing.

That first email sent me down the content marketing path that brought in $4 million in sales over the first year.

And you thought email was dead.

It's not even close.

So I thought it was best to start with "Why."

Why email (and the content you create from it) is the best way to turn Internet leads into paying clients who contact you first?

Here is my answer.

Why email is the best place to start with marketing

This is my personal opinion and the main reason why I prefer email first for Internet leads.

Now, I'm not saying that you shouldn't call your clients or that you shouldn't advertise. I am suggesting that you should first email your online leads and then implement your other marketing around it.

Most people hate talking on the phone, especially to those they view as sales people.

Don't get me wrong. If you already have a warm relationship, an urgent need, or if they ask you to call them, pick up the phone.

This is not an Anti-Telephone rant. It is really about building relationships versus annoyance marketing.

Like I said, most people hate telemarketing calls (yes, that's how they view you if you cold call). Most people are too busy to be interrupted.

The bar is low in real estate, especially when it comes to Internet leads. Most agents are going to take one of three routes with a lead.

The first route would be to simply ignore the lead. It's hard to believe that some agents spend money marketing and do not work the leads. Nevertheless, this happens everyday. This might be 50% of the agents. I can't even call this the low bar.

The second route would be to set you up on a drip email. Or even better, a listing alert. It sounds so exciting! I'm getting dripped! I'm getting alerts for properties that I'm not interested in. This is the low bar set for you. Maybe 40% of the agents fall in this category.

The third route, the last 10%, will call you until you tell them to stop or take out a restraining order. I appreciate their persistence, but annoying people into doing business with you is not why I got into real estate. You might get a lot of business with the telephone. Though, it comes with it's share of headaches and disappointments.

Only a small few, like you, will do email and content marketing the right way by treating people like family and starting relationships online that lead to clients.

When done the right way, email is an efficient, non-intrusive way to start building a relationship with many people at the same time.

When you write emails like I teach in this book, people will start to know, like, and trust you through what you have to say when you consistently show up in their inbox.

Instead of high pressure sales tactics or goofy recipes, you will be entertaining them with stories, teaching them about real estate, and demonstrating why you are the best one to work with.

Compared to your competition, you will stick out like a diamond in a coal store.

You will attract people who you want to do business with and filter out those who would drive you crazy and waste your time

The Filter Factor

If you are like me, you prefer to work with clients who are ready, willing, and able to work with you. These are called 5 Star Prospects. We will talk more about these 5 Star Prospects in the chapter on "How to Convert Leads."

One of the beautiful parts of this system is the built-in filter.

As people receive your emails over time, they will either decide that they relate to what you have to say or they don't.

And that's ok.

We all have different personalities. That's just they way we are designed. And it makes the world much more interesting and much less boring.

Due to these differences, it's natural that individuals are attracted to some personalities and repelled by others.

When you show your authentic personality in your writing, others notice that intrinsically. As they learn more about you, they will automatically drift toward you or away from you.

Don't take this personally. Especially when people complain or unsubscribe from your list.

When they leave, they are doing you both a favor.

This process of filtering prevents you from driving each other crazy.

No one wants a bad experience.

Learn that it's ok when someone unsubscribes and realize that your system is working for you.

Occasionally, you will discover someone who needs to take action immediately and just signed up for your list.

If they need to take action right now, then help them if you can. Just realize that they don't know, like, or trust you yet.

These "fast" clients may have been your favorite leads in the past, but that will likely change as this marketing system works for you over time.

Email = Leverage

I know of no other way that you connect with so many people in a very personal (yet non-intrusive) way at such a low cost.

Note: This is coming from a guy who was successful selling over the phone in three different industries.

Even if you like what I said, don't take my word. It's just my opinion.

So...

Let's take a look at a successful email campaign and other studies so you can come to your own conclusion.

Also keep in mind our goal in nurturing: To START building relationships online that leads to business offline.

This book is the online phase of the lead conversion. I will show you how to get from online to in-person—a way to move from Screen2Screen to Face2Face.

2012 Obama Email Campaign

This was one of the most successful email campaigns in history.

Obama's team raised $690 million from more than 4.5 million donors in just a few months. More importantly, he gained a huge audience of true supporters who propelled him to a second term when all the odds were against him.

This is what we all want: A legion of dedicated people who champion your cause and business.

This example is not meant to be a political statement. Love him or hate him, you must respect the job his team did building relationships with their voters (audience) online.

They told stories and connected them to the election in order to get people to take action.

They sent emails almost every day. The frequency increased as the election drew near. The team kept testing and kept sending because it worked.

They also discovered that people like clarity in their emails. A call to action is OK, but if they smell a trick, they feel betrayed.

This occurred to me after breaking down many of the messages. Their emails looked like something you might receive from a close friend or family member.

This is an important study because their top goal was identical to ours, to start building relationships online that lead to action later.

Recent Studies

A recent study by the California Association of Realtors [CAR] showed that most people prefer fewer phone calls and more digital communications with their agent.

Another study by Hubspot, a leading Marketing Technology Company, showed:

- 91% of consumers check their email daily
- 74% of consumers prefer to receive commercial communications via email
- 50%+ of emails are opened on mobile devices (make sure your email is mobile ready)

Why Not Text?

Text is less personal and harder to tell a story.

Texting has a place in lead conversion, though I think it's most powerful for transactional messages with those who are closer to taking action.

Keep it Simple

Albert Einstein said it best, "Everything must be made as simple as possible. But not simpler."

Complex systems tend to fail over time due to the human factor. These systems have a higher front-end learning curve. People tend to shortcut a difficult system. Complex systems need more oversight and create an unhappy work environment. They are more costly to implement and maintain.

You don't want to automatically sacrifice efficiency for simplicity.

In these cases, weigh the costs versus the benefits and make the best decision for you and your business.

This marketing system is designed to be simple and flexible. It can be used with as little or as much technology as you want. In the last chapter, I show you the tech and tools I personally used to sell $4 million in homes.

Tips and Tricks

- This system will only work on an audience who has opted-in to your list. In other words, they have signed up to receive your emails. Emailing people you have added to the list (without their permission) is spamming. Don't SPAM. It is annoying and will not bring you the results that you desire.
- Emailing frequently increases engagement and helps build trust.

- Emailing frequently moves you from expert to authority in the eyes of your audience.
- Emailing frequently enhances your writing skills and makes you more persuasive.
- Emails should be about entertaining stories that you can connect to your business to increase engagement and build relationships.
- When done right, people will look forward to your emails, like they do their favorite show or series.
- Do not worry about those who unsubscribe, they were not likely to buy from you anyway.
- If they are written in your "own voice," those who don't "get" you will unsubscribe. This is a good thing.
- Your emails should look like a message they receive from someone they know and not an advertisement. Most people are not doing email this way, so you will stand out against your competition.
- Time Block your creative/writing time. I set aside time every day to write the email. It takes about 15 minutes for me right now, and you will get faster over time.
- Email is fast and (nearly) free!

Ready to Start?

In the next section, we are going to discuss knowing your market. It is the most important thing you will do to be successful with marketing.

I believe that in any business endeavor, you should always start with your audience. It is impossible to grab their attention and get them hooked if you don't know what drives them and what keeps them up at night.

The path from thinking about real estate to taking action can be a long process. To build relationships, it is helpful for you to understand your client's mindset at every point along the path.

Then, we will start to break down the structure of the email, explain the purpose of each part, and learn what you need to do to build relationships through email. It's an extensive study on story telling and using them to get people to take action.

Finally, we will wrap this up by sharing the tools that I use and the systems I put in place to produce content, promote it to my audience, nurture leads, and generate clients.

Let's do this!

1
Know Your Audience and Market

"The aim of marketing is to know and understand the customer so well the product or service fits him and sells itself."

~ Peter Drucker - Author, Educator and the founder of modern business management

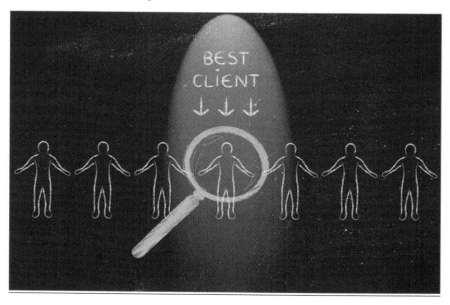

Start With Your Audience

Once upon a time, an archer wanted to perfect his craft. So, he looked far and wide for a master archer to study. After some time he came across an arrow in a tree in the woods. This arrow was in the exact center of a three-ring bullseye.

As he continued down the trail towards the next town, he found them everywhere. The archer's excitement grew because he thought that he had found his master.

When he got to town, he asked where he could find the man responsible for all of the bullseyes.

He was taken to a small workshop on the edge of town. Inside was an ancient craftsman finishing one of the arrows.

The archer asked the craftsman how he hits the center each time. The craftsman said, " Watch this," and he went outside.

The craftsman took the new arrow placed it in the bow and shot it into the side of the tree.

He then picked up a can of paint and painted the bullseye around the arrow.

It's important that before you begin marketing that you start with your audience. You learn about their goals, fears, desires, and interests. You learn everything that you can, so that you can relate to them with your marketing and advertising.

The more you know about your audience, the easier it is to hit a bullseye.

What if you do not have an audience? (or it's really small)

In this case, you would target your market like the ancient craftsman.

You let your personality shine in your emails and your audience grows by those who relate to and connect to you. Your emails and communications will paint those lines for you. They form the target around your arrow.

Researching Your Audience

Before you write a single word, you need to know your market inside and out. When I say "your market", I am referring to the buyers, sellers, trends, problems, issues, competitors, and your solutions.

There are many ways of doing this and you should dive deep before hitting send on the first email. Even if you do not have an email list, you still need to understand the big picture of your market and information on typical clients at a minimum.

You should not skimp on time or your commitment to this system. Often, market research is what makes or breaks your sales efforts.

If you do not understand what your clients desire, know what they fear, and how to solve their problems, then you will connect with fewer people and write less effective emails. Just as importantly, you won't repel those who drive you crazy.

In the next section, I will give you a list of questions you need answered in your research. When done right, you will get the answers and many unexpected bonuses along the way.

Memorize these market research questions. They will come in handy when doing research, and when interacting with potential clients.

You never know when some one is going to give or point you to one of the answers, so stay on your toes. When you stumble onto one of these "easter eggs" write it down quickly or make a digital note.

Here's where to look for answers to the market research questions:

- Online forums - through observation and discussion
- Networking with Public - through observation and discussion
- Competition - through discussion and secret shopping
- Your Best Clients - through discussion and questionnaires
- Professional Surveys/Profiles - from NAR or local associations.

Market Research Questions to Ask and Find Answers

The answers to these questions are imperative to your success. Market research is a never-ending assignment because your market is constantly in flux. Keep searching for these answers and the many changes that affect your market.

Questions for your market, clients and customers

- Who are your clients and prospects?
- Tell me everything you can about your clients?
- What are their biggest challenges? With buying and selling?
- What do they fear?
- What do they want to accomplish?
- Describe a typical day in your client's life?
- What is the urgency in their minds for buying/selling?
- What are their obstacles to buying/selling?
- What are they angry at?
- What are they insecure about?
- How does that affect them?
- What emotions are going through their head?
- What are their dreams?
- What do they need to hear?
- How do they view the local economy?
- How do they view the local real estate market?

The Customer Persona

Once you have all of the market research completed and questions answered, you are left with a "persona." A marketing persona is one person or character who embodies a collection of ideas and personalities.

This persona can be symbolized by a fictitious person who is created from the marketing materials or based on a real live human being.

What's important is that you can picture this persona in your mind's eye and write to them when you are cranking out an email. Just like you would to a friend or family member.

Use the information you gathered in your market research. When you write about your client's fears, desires and concerns, you will connect on a deeper, emotional level.

The beauty of a persona is that it helps you write in a conversational style that is very personal.

It's much different that when you are writing to a group.

Sub-consciously your mind picks up these clues and uses them to filter out what is not important. When you read a message written only to you, your mind gives that a higher priority.

I know this sounds weird, but go into your email. Compare something that you wrote to one person to another email that you wrote to a group.

Can you see the difference? Did you feel the difference?

Write with Authenticity

Your emails should show your own personality, not a second-rate version of someone else.

[Unless of course, you are ghost writing for another person]

I would think this would come natural to most people, but it does not. I'll blame it on the proliferation of grammar cops and our own insecurities.

Not everyone speaks like William Shakespeare. So let's not try to copy his style or that of any other person.

Let's try to keep this really simple.

Write like you talk – the good, the bad and the ugly.

Your emails should be written with a WYSIWYG mentality. [What You See Is What You Get]

Your clients need to see the real you in your emails. The need to see what you love, what you stand for, what you stand against, your passions, your principles, and even some of your failures. No matter what personality you have in real life, there are people attracted to it.

This is how some people come to know and like you before they ever meet you in person. This is how people know you are real.

When you write like you talk in real life, there are no surprises when you come belly to belly for the first time. The personality they learned to love online is on full display in real life.

Know, Like, and Trust

You've heard that people buy from those who they know, like, and trust.

And it is true.

When you write with authenticity, people will get to know the real you. Some people will naturally gravitate toward you when you write with your own personality. These people likely share some of your ideals, values, and passions.

If you write to them long enough, then...

Those who don't relate will likely unsubscribe.

But those who "get" you will hang around because they like you.

Now that we have our arms around the "know and like," how do people learn to trust you through email?

Most psychologists agree that trust is built with things like generosity, patience, dependability, consistency and transparency.

When you type "My Realtor" in Google, the first suggestion is "My Realtor never calls me." Sadly enough, this is the prevalent thought about agents in America.

What kind of impression do you think it could make if you were in their inbox every weekday, before they had to reach out to you. What would they think if you did this for months on end?

Instead of sending them listings they didn't ask for or your granny's favorite rhubarb recipe, you sent them something they valued.

That could be an entertaining story that answered a question in the back of their mind or your expert perspective on a troubling situation.

These are your opportunities to build trust with email.

Discovering the Real You

Unless we are completely self-aware, many people don't see themselves the same way others do.

So a little introspection is a good idea, if you haven't done this recently.

We all change as we go through life, so if you did this more than a few years ago, I suggest that you do not skip this exercise.

Here are some questions you can ask yourself about you and your business

- What are your weaknesses? And of the business?
- What are you afraid to admit about your business?
- What are your short, medium, and long-term goals?
- What are your biggest challenges?
- What are the benefits of working with your business?
- If you had unlimited powers, what would you change in your business?

- What do you do better than your competition?
- Why are you the best person to solve your client's problem?
- What are you most passionate about in life?
- What are your core values?

Gathering your thoughts by answering these questions helps you write with authenticity.

Conversion Theory

A wise man once said, "To convert somebody go to them, take them by the hand and guide them."

The man who said this was St. Thomas Aquinas.

Now, don't think I'm trying to beat you over the head with a religion because I think this theory is just as true in lead conversion.

Most people don't wake up one day and take action on buying or selling their home. Real Estate is a long sales cycle. From the first thought to closing escrow is typically between six months and two years.

And when someone first signs up to your list, you don't know if they are just starting to look, ready to take action, or somewhere in between.

There is a pathway that most people follow on their way to buying or selling a home. Everyone's path is slightly different and that's ok. Because once we know where they are, we can help show them where they want to go.

So, part of your job is to discover the location on the path for each of your leads. Once you know their location, it is easier to start to connect with them because you will have an understanding of their mindset. You should know what concerns and questions people typically have at this point.

This is what St. Thomas meant by "going to them." You are going to where they are mentally and where they are on this path to buying or selling a home.

He also said take "them by the hand and guide them." I see that as customer education, entertaining information, expert advice, and showing them the way to where they want to go.

This is how I hold their hand and then guide them to the closing table.

Another thing to consider is the speed of their pace. Some people take baby steps while others are in a full-on sprint. There is a time and place for both, and they will need your guidance here too.

Online Conversion Pathway

Before we go further, I want to make sure that I do not confuse you. In the section above we discussed a pathway for buying or selling real estate. In other words, all the little steps that people take in order to complete a transaction.

In this section, we will discuss the steps that people take on the way to choosing an agent. This is a conversion pathway for those who find their agent online.

Although, everyone's path in real estate is a little different, we can start to guide them once we know where they are on the conversion pathway.

Keep in mind that people change their mindset as they move through the conversion pathway. What is important to them today is different from yesterday or tomorrow. To avoid confusion, it's best to stick with the questions that they have right now. Focus on answering their current concerns and moving them along the path.

Most clients will not take action if there is any confusion or unanswered questions. So, it's best to take them one step at a time.

The Online Conversion Pathway

5-Star Prospects

In addition to knowing where they are on the conversion pathway, you also want to qualify your clients to see if they meet certain standards.

My basic standards for potential customers follows what Joe Polish calls 5 Star Prospects. In addition to being a best selling author and speaker, Joe knows a thing or two about marketing. He helps entrepreneurs and Fortune 500 companies generate massive numbers of leads and sales.

A 5 Star Prospect is someone who is:
1. Willing to Communicate
2. Friendly and Cooperative
3. Know what they want
4. Knows when they want it
5. Wants us to help them

In the last chapter, I discuss how to use the 5 Star System to qualify and convert more leads to clients.

2
How to Add Value

"When he drives a car off the lot, its price increases in value"
~ Dos Equis' *The Most Interesting Man in the World.*

Have you ever noticed that everyone tells you to add value in your content, and no one tells you how to do it?

Well, they might give you examples of things that add value. However, you are left without the tools necessary to do this with consistency.

Most of us are left with the impression that information adds value and that we should create content that is full of information.

This is why the average agent (if they are creating content) is writing about home maintenance tips and the best way to stage your home.

But information on it's own is boring. And most people don't automatically think it is valuable because most of it is free and easy to accesses on the Internet.

You don't need to receive an email about home staging because you can google a million articles in just a few seconds.

If you want to know what people value, just follow the money. People will tell you what they think you want to hear, but the money never lies.

Most people would agree that the highest paid professionals in America today are entertainers, attorneys and doctors.

So, what do they have in common?

These professionals provide entertainment or expert advice for serious problems.

Like the Dos Equis man, being interesting is the easiest way to get attention and add value to your work. Below I've given you three ways to become a more interesting content creator.

Here are three ways you can add value to the content your create

1. Provide expert advice to your audience
2. Tell stories that follow a theme that your audience will recognize
3. Tell entertaining stories

What I like to do is combine entertainment and expert advice with relatable stories into an atomic value bomb that blows their mind and has them coming back for more.

Your clients want to learn about the market and real estate, but they do not want to know every detail. It's best to give them enough information to make a good decision without boring or confusing them. You also don't want to give them so much information that they think they can solve the problem on their own. This is true in the content that you create and when interacting with them personally.

We will dive into telling stories that your audience finds interesting and entertaining in the chapter on storytelling.

For now, we are going to focus on story themes. Themes are like story patterns that your mind recognizes. If the pattern is familiar to you, it's likely that it will catch your attention and make you read further.

The audience wants to see if the story will turn out like they expect. These types of stories help us to find meaning in this shared experience that we call life.

To help, I've categorized several story themes that you can use over and over in your emails to entertain your prospects and demonstrate your expertise. To keep your audience from getting bored, I recommend using a variety of themes.

As you work your way through the email template and the appendix, you will find examples of each of these themes and why they work.

No one has influenced my email writing style more than Ben Settle, a world leader in email copywriting education. Ben's shocking writing style and his ability to connect with his audience are paramount to his success in business. Some of his story theme ideas are included in the list below.

Story Themes that Add Value

- **Inspirational**
  Real Estate is a tough business. It is easy for people to get discouraged and give up at just the wrong time. All of us need inspiration from time to time in order to take action. And by action, we want them to take the next step on the conversion pathway. Sometimes all they need is a little nudge. So, tell stories that inspire you and find a way to connect it to your business.

- **Origin Stories**

    Origin stories are the back stories to our life that explain where we came from, why we do what we do and how we obtained our expertise. These stories help explain our purpose in helping others and give confidence that we can do the same for them. In addition to getting a peek behind the curtain, origin stories are entertaining because they satisfy our deep longing for knowing why things are the way they are.

- **Shocking**

    Shocking stories gets people's attention. As a safety feature, our subconscious brain puts a priority on problem situations. Because they look so different from everything else in our inbox, they can be impossible to ignore. Use the power of weird and bizarre stories to grab the attention of your audience and answer their concerns.

- **Demonstration**

    You can demonstrate your value to others by telling a story how you successfully helped a client solve their problems. Problem solving is one area where people look to us the most, so it is imperative that they understand you can help. Just telling them that you can help them is not enough. In lieu of a testimonial, stories of how you helped someone are the best way to show your audience that you are the one they want to work with.

- **Pop Culture**

    People are attracted to pop culture because it helps us to connect to the broader world and we find part of our shared identity in it. We use pop culture to make statements about who we are and more importantly, who we are not. It's really interesting to see lessons tied to our favorite characters and shows. Use pop culture to share your identity and connect with your audience on another level.

- **Current Events**
  Current events are much like pop culture in the way we connect to each other. These events are shared experiences where we find identity and learn about each other in new ways. We use these experiences to do the heavy lifting of entertaining while we educate and solve problems.

- **Conflicting Information**
  When your brain recognizes conflicting information it causes a form of stress or mental discomfort. This information could be ideas, beliefs or values. Psychologists call this cognitive dissonance. When we experience dissonance in a headline we strive to resolve the internal dilemma by reading the rest of the article. We hope to find a reason to justify the imbalance or a change in behavior. So, it's important that there is some resolution in your story to fully satisfy the reader.

- **Taking a Stand**
  I don't recommend this strategy for the sake of using it. Only take a stand when you fully believe in it and the prevailing wisdom is wrong. You've probably seen someone fake this tactic before and it comes off as weird. When done right this is very compelling. It creates curiosity and

helps people get to know you through your values and beliefs. Making a case against something sets you apart from the competition.

- **Social Proof**

    Social proof is another way to demonstrate your value to your prospects. Instead of telling them a story about solving a real estate problem for another client, you could have one of your clients tell the story for you. When done properly, testimonials can be a strong form of social proof. Or your story could be told through the authority of another well known company or individual. It's easier to learn to trust if they can relate you to something they are familiar with.

- **Answering Questions**

    Until all their questions are answered, clients are in a state of confusion and can't move forward. They are stuck in place until all their concerns are satisfied. These type of questions can come from your clients, your colleagues or real estate forums online. If one person you know has this concern, there are others who feel the same way.

3
The Email Pattern

"Like a path through the woods, patterns help your audience find their way to the end of the story"

~ Steve Jolly

Every story has a pattern or structure. If you study them long enough you will see these structures repeat from one story (or movie) to the next. For example, if you are a Star Wars fan, you probably noticed that the plot in the last movie is the same as the plot in the original movie.

It starts in an ordinary place with an unexpected hero. This hero receives a call to adventure that they reluctantly refuse. Then they meet their mentor and decide to heed the call. The hero overcomes obstacles, gathers allies and fights enemies. They have a major problem that requires a sacrifice (on their part) to solve. The enemy is defeated, and they reap the rewards of becoming the hero no one expected.

Maybe, Star Wars is not your thing. Think about The Wizard of Oz, Finding Nemo, The Matrix, The Incredibles, O Brother Where Art Thou, The Lord of the Rings, The Silence of the Lambs, Avatar and hundreds of other movies and stories. They all follow a similar pattern.

This pattern is called the Monomyth or The Hero's Journey and it is not the only one. There are many story patterns that work. The trick is finding (or developing) one that works for you.

Since stories are a huge part of how we will nurture our prospects, our emails need a structure too. This pattern is what works for my style of writing. I recommend that you start with this structure. Feel free to use it to guide your writing. With experience you can change it to best fit your needs.

My email marketing pattern has five parts. It is designed for use in telling the type of short stories that you might write in an email: The Headline [Subject], Opening, Story, Sell and Closing. Each section has a specific purpose. When put together properly, they help you to increase engagement, build relationships with your prospects, and further relationships with friends/clients.

Below you will find an overview of each section. In the upcoming chapters, we will look at each section of the template in more detail with examples.

Headline

The headline is the subject line of the email. The ultimate goal of the headline is to capture people's attention so they open your email. Writing headlines is an art. You have a limited amount of words to capture someone's attention and set the theme for the email.

So...

Every Word Counts.Like story patterns, headlines can also be categorized by type. Some are designed for shock effect, to arouse curiosity, to show you the benefit, tied to current events, or to showcase a list of items.

What you want to do is to use emotion and curiosity in your headline to create fascination with your audience. Fascination (like indecency) is one of those things that is hard to measure, but you know it when you see it.

Opening

If the headline is designed to grab people's attention, then the goal of the opening is to hook your audience so they will read through to the end of your story. In the type of emails that I write, the opening is the first few sentences that follow the headline.

Therefore, if you are into fishing, this analogy will help you understand. The bait is like the headline (That's why the worst headlines are called "Click Bait"). It gets the audience to open the email and take the bait.

The opening is like setting the hook in the fish after they take the bait. The beginning needs to be so intriguing that the audience cannot put it down. They are literally hooked on finding out what happens in the story.

Time to reel them in.

Story

The story is the main idea or information that you want to say to your audience. Your Goal is to relate, entertain and educate. It can be anything as long as you can connect it to yourself and the audience.

Whatever you decide to say, you need to talk about it in an interesting way. In your own voice and personality. It's not teaching or training or pure information.

Think Infotainment.

Anyone can put out information. On its own, information gets boring fast.

When you entertain, share the big picture, and make them smile; you are building relationships. You are seen as a leader and someone they want to follow.

Sell

The sell is where you pivot from the story to the relationship with your audience and you ask for the sale (Call to Action). Your goal is to get them to take action by connecting to them emotionally.

How the story can connect to your audience:
- Feature of your business
- Benefit of working with you
- Something fascinating about you, your area or your business
- A problem the audience is likely to have
- A pain the audience is likely to feel.
- An obstacle the audience is likely to face
- An insecurity the audience is likely to have

These connections can be direct or implied. Use that connection to prepare them for the Call to Action [CTA].

The CTA is what you say to your audience to get them to take a specific action. Your ultimate goal is to get them to take actions which leads to a relationship with you.

The call to action could be in many forms. For a physical product, it could be a Buy Now or Add to Cart Button. Links to forms and landing pages are commonly found in CTAs.

Since we are building relationships (and not selling products), my typical CTA is a mini sales pitch with question or a request for them to hit reply. One CTA is usually best here. Fewer choices lead to less confusion. Don't sell your self short and use seduction to create the best calls to action.

Close

The Close is how you wrap up your email. The goal with the close is to leave your audience with a smile and maybe more.

Some folks close with a second CTA. In my weekday email to my audience, I close with the Deal of the Day. It is a vague description of a value property with a link to the listing on my website. Not everyone on your list is ready for a conversation; this helps them find their way back to your website.

You can also use the close to build trust, show social proof, or tease another benefit.

Tips and Tricks

- Mail daily (or weekly at a minimum) to increase engagement and relationship building. Less email doesn't produce more relationships and sales.
- Email length should be about 200 – 600 words. Occasionally, you can send longer emails, but many people will not read them.
- Use a mobile friendly HTML template that looks like plain text so you can track clicks and opens and not look spammy.

- The theme of the email runs like a thread from the beginning to the end of the email.
- Variety in themes, styles and story types keeps your audience interested.

4
Headlines

"On the average, five times as many people read the headline as read the body copy. When you have written your headline, you have spent eighty cents out of your dollar."

~ David Ogilvy, founder of world famous advertising firm, Ogilvy & Mather and recognized as the father of advertising.

Ogilvy worked in a time before email and computers. And in media that was very expensive: live television, magazine and direct mail.

If his headlines failed, he could potentially lose millions of dollars for his clients.

Ogilvy knew that a headline is your first impression. If you blow it, no one will take the time to read your story. This is why headlines are more important than the story.

In an email, the headline is the subject line. The primary goal of the headline is to get people to open your email. It's that simple.

Then again, it's not that simple.

Writing headlines is an art. You have a limited amount of words to capture someone's attention and set the theme for the email. In order to get someone to open your email, they need to be fascinated by the headline.

Fascination (or curiosity) can be created by referencing something that intrigues your audience. At a minimum, it needs to be something that they have seen, heard, observed or thought. When it's something they are familiar with, the audience knows that this story is for them.

Many times this fascination will come in the form of an analogy, metaphor, simile, or play on words. It is not a requirement that it falls into one of these categories. When done right, this works to connect people to the (boring) info that you want to present with something entertaining and interesting.

You need more than just curiosity to get more people to read the body of your email. You also need to connect emotionally.

Great Headlines = Curiosity + Emotion
So how are you going to connect emotionally?

Problems (and Solutions)...

People are attracted to problems like a moth to a flame. It's our subconscious mind that moves problems to the top of our attention list.

By addressing a specific problem we force people to stop what they are doing and consider what we have to say.

Problems are one of the few things that break through the noise of information that blows through our lives daily.

Problems alone are not enough to create the emotion we want people to feel. A problem only becomes compelling when you show a solution and why you are the best one to help them solve their problems.

Problems also make us think, especially about the future.

Scientist call this "episodic future thinking" or prospection.

Recent research indicates that people can experience intense emotional reactions when thinking about the future that can influence behavior. They also found that the intensity is highest with thoughts of the future, then thoughts of the past, followed by a "meh" for the present.

And that's why great selling agents want people to be able to imagine what it's like to live in this home. And why car salesman want you to sit behind the wheel of a car in the showroom.

Picturing what it's like to own it, makes you want it that much more.

These are just some of the reasons why great headlines are key to your success.

The Theme

Before you start writing, it is best to decide the theme of the email. This theme will run from the headline to the close (like a thread). Since the theme is represented in the headline, some find it is easiest to start with the theme.

Another reason you need this consistent theme from subject line to close is trust. If you promise them one thing in the headline and then do not deliver, then you are eroding your trust with each email.

It's like a bait and switch with every click.

Who wants that kind of experience?

The government (both state and federal) doesn't look kindly on these misleading practices either.

It's best for the headline to set the theme which creatively flows like a thread all the way to the close.

Trust is delivered in the consistency of your message and the consistency in delivery. It takes time to develop. If you consistently show up and bring something of value, you will gradually build trust.

Headline Analysis

Once I decide on the theme of the story, I will write 10 – 20 headlines to see which one I like best. Look for the ones that tug on your emotions. You will know it when you see it.

I might even run them through a headline analyzer to see how they score emotionally.

http://coschedule.com/headline-analyzer

http://www.aminstitute.com/headline/index.htm

The Coschedule Headline Analyzer works best for checking the headlines of emails and blog posts. This tool analyzes the types of words used and in what context. It's designed for the shorter headlines you find in these types of media.

The Headline Analyzer at the American Marketing Institute is a great all around tool that can work with longer headlines like you might find in a sales letter. It primarily looks at the number of power/emotional words used and what category they fall under. There is no contextual scoring.

As for analyzing the level of curiosity, we are still waiting on that. These heading analyzers help you get started, after some time you won't need to use them and testing will become more important for effective headlines.

Once the email is complete, I will circle back to the headline to dial it in.

Headlines can come in many shapes and forms. Here are some common themes that I use in headlines (and stories too). Notice that the headline might fall into two or more of the categories listed. When this happens, it helps you relate to a broader audience.

Headline Examples by Theme

- Inspirational
    - After 959 failures she said, never give up
    - How one simple act can create something amazing
    - The Nashville bear who restored faith in people.

- Origin Stories
    - This was the wakeup call I never wanted
    - Why I became a Realtor (and it's not what you think)
    - Why I never wear green on St. Patricks Day.

- Shocking
    - The Bizarre Antics of House Hunting TV
    - What a Bizarre Choice to Top this List
    - Doomed from the Start.

- Demonstration
    - The Secret to Our Success

- How the Fed Rate Hike will Affect the Nashville Market?
- How to Find Value in Any Market.

- Pop Culture
    - Survey Says...
    - She Bought a Ticket to Ride
    - One Man's Trash is another Man's $500,000.

- Current Events
    - Hot Chicken on a Brexit
    - The Moneyball Strategy for Nashville Real Estate
    - The Secret to Saban's Success.

- Conflicting Information
    - A falling appraisal in a rising market
    - The fate of "Nashville" is up in the air
    - Short Term Rentals: A Nashville gold mine or a bottomless pit.

- Taking a Stand
    - They only look like an overnight success
    - Why the Experts are Wrong about the Holidays
    - Buyers are liars, even in Mayberry.

- Social Proof
    - How Taylor Swift bought her latest Nashville home
    - Three rules of highly effective organizations by the Special Forces
    - Make your mark like a Manning.

- Answering Questions
    - I always get this question
    - What's your home really worth?
    - The question every Nashville homeowner asks

Examples of Real-Life Boring Headlines

Do Not Use These Unless You Want No Audience!

These are actual headlines that I received from other Real Estate Agents.

Unless you had a strong connection to the sender, why would anyone open these emails?

- Open House Flyer 2 Blue
- Tidbits from Your Friend 4 Life
- Monthly Newsletter January 2016
- My New Listing*MMG Weekly: Thanksgiving Holiday
- Village of Old Hickory Charmer
- West Meade Hills Property
- New Listing in Nolensville
- A Winter Recipe*Wine and Cheese Open House
- John's Bolognese/Ragu Sauce
- Homes and Money Newsletter – 3rd Quarter

Headline Inspiration

If you get stuck writing headlines, there are many places you can go for inspiration. When I say inspiration, I am not talking about cut and paste. You might find a word that evokes the perfect emotion or a style/template that you can emulate.

- Google Image Search – Cosmopolitan and other similar magazine covers
- Swiped.com
- Other Successful Ads from Copywriters
- Formulas or templates
- Books on Copywriting
- Sites like Copyblogger.com

Tips and Tricks

- Make sure the theme of the story is reflected in the headline.
- The headline is more important than the story. Take time to create a good one.
- Don't steal someone's headline, instead be inspired by it.
- Don't mislead. No bait and switch headlines.
- Make the headline pay off quickly in the email. Deliver on your promise.

5
The Opening

"Every great introduction creates shock or seduction."

~ Steve Jolly

The goal of the opening is similar to the goal of the headline. However, we want to do more than get their attention. We want to hook the audience so they want to read the rest of the story. If you do not catch the attention of your audience quickly, they will get bored and move on.

The opening of your story is much like an introduction. First impressions are essential in getting them to the end. And if they don't get to the end of the story, it's nearly impossible to get them to "buy in" and take action.

Check this out. According to a recent study by Microsoft, we now have a shorter attention span than a goldfish. It's currently at eight seconds.

That's right. Eight Seconds. Maybe Less with Email.

So you better get them thinking quickly.

Good openings raise questions and set the mood for the story.

Good openings follow the theme established in the headline.

Good openings begin with tension and immediacy.

As with all good writing, there are some patterns that you can follow.

Here's a few to look at.

Examples of Story Openings by Theme

- **Inspirational** - Most people think that the holidays are a terrible time to buy a home. And I would have to vehemently disagree with them. The biggest obstacle that you have to getting the best deal are the other buyers who are willing to pay more for the same home.

- **Origin Stories** - If you've heard me talk about my start in real estate, you probably heard me say it had to do with the opportunity that I saw in selling bank-owned homes. This opportunity was not the reason "Why" I decided to become a Realtor, it was simply my vehicle for entering the real estate industry in a way that made sense for me.
- **Shocking** - Everyone in Tennessee has heard about the Curse of the Bell Witch. This story is part the early settlement history of Middle Tennessee and is the most famous, local legend. The epicenter of the curse is John Bell's Farm located along the Red River in Adams, Tennessee.
- **Demonstration** - Most people will not believe me when I say this, but there is value to be found in the Nashville Real Estate Market. I was reminded of the value in Nashville as I was reviewing the numbers of a foreclosure auction that I attended yesterday.
- **Pop Culture** - Stan Caffy was a local pipefitter who liked to look for odd and old things, especially at garage sales. In the mid-nineties he found an old, stained parchment of the Declaration of Independence and paid $2 for it. He purchased it to hang in his Donelson garage where Stan liked to work on bikes.
- **Current Events** - I've held off on writing about the Brexit until the dust settled and calmer heads prevailed. The stock dumping tsunami subsided on Tuesday when bargain hunters flooded the exchanges to scoop up deals. And we are seeing the same thing happening today. Like most, you are probably wondering how this change in European politics will affect the Nashville market.

- **Conflicting Information** - Short term rentals like AirBnB and VRBO have become all of the rage for investors lately due to the amount of money some are making with this strategy. Many things have changed in Nashville since the short term rental market exploded here a few years ago.
- **Taking a Stand** - Most "so called" experts will tell you that the holidays are a bad time to sell your home. That you should wait until Spring. That no one sells their home during the holidays. It is dangerous to give this kind of "one size fits all" advice.
- **Social Proof** - Yesterday, I told you about Tennessee State Senator Mark Green. He came to speak at a meeting about leading highly effective organizations, and all I told you about was his interview with Saddam Hussein the night he was captured in Iraq.
- **Answering Questions** - One of the first things you do when you are thinking about selling your home is to determine the value of your home. The "true" value is determined by what a ready, willing and able buyer will pay for your home. But, we want to know the value before we put it on the market.

Other Common Opening Themes for Stories

- **Setting the Scene** – (time, location, context, and atmosphere) "It was 1941. We were in a pub in London."
- **In the middle of conflict** – "They lost him twice in the chopper ride back to Camp Bastion."

- **Mysterious Situations** – (The Unusual and Unexpected) - "His house at Crystal Lake was dark and its windows were blacker than his eyes"

- **Narrator talking to the audience** – "Once upon a time, in a far away land, there was a tiny kingdom"

- **Quotation** – Seth Godin says, "You're either remarkable or invisible."

Study the Openings of Other Stories

If your ideal clients are similar to you, study the opening of your favorite books, stories and movies. Pay attention to the words they use and the patterns of their writing.

If you are trying to attract a different audience, study the openings of their favorite material.

When you use something that is familiar it will attract the right audience, your ideal clients.

Don't be a jerk by swiping and stealing other people's ideas. Instead, use these openings as inspiration or templates for your writing.

Tips and Tricks

- Email is a short story format. Get them hooked and into the story quickly.

- Variety is key to keeping the audience interested over the long run

- Look at a story through the eyes of the problem

- Get to the problem quickly

- Make sure the opening flows with the theme and the story
- Get right into the action
- Think about which Point of View to tell the story? 1st, 2nd or 3rd Person

6
The Story

"Marketing is no longer about the stuff that you make, but about the stories you tell."

~ Seth Godin - Best selling author, marketer and speaker.

Good storytelling sometimes breaks the rules. There is not one right way to tell a story. The future success of a story cannot be measured or proven in any scientific way. Yet, we know a good story when we see it.

The story is where the magic happens. That magic is what we call influence. Stories influence others because it's a way to speak to their heart and paint a picture so clear that they see it too.

Information is boring. It's a commodity. They can get it anywhere.

Some of the best stories are about you. They are personal. They help people build faith in you and your business.

You can't tell them to have faith. They have to make that conclusion themselves. You have to inspire them to believe. You have to lead them to the water, but they have to decide to drink.

People value their own conclusions over anything they are told. You have to earn their trust. They have to find faith.

Once they believe in you, they begin to tell your story.

This is how faith, trust and influence are born.

Types Of Stories That Influence and Build Trust

Who I Am and Why I Am Here

These two stories are essential in order to gain trust. People want to do business with those they know, like and trust. These two questions are essential in order to build faith and gain influence. In fact, most people will not listen to you until they know you are important.

These questions also start to define your persona, your image in the eyes of the consumer. To be most effective when you write, it is essential that you fully understand who you are and your ideal clients. It's less about what we say and more about how we say it. If you don't show them who you are and what you stand for, they will likely make it up on their own. And that's not good for any of us.

Vision

The Vision Story is where you inspire your audience by showing them how they will benefit from working with you. People want to feel good about themselves and the choices they are making. When you make people feel good about themselves, they will start to feel good about you too.

Challenge people to look at themselves and strive to be better.

Inspiration leads to action. Find out what inspires you (and your audience) and talk about it.

Teaching

Teaching is a valid need in our business. Teaching clients helps streamline the counseling process, better prepares them for the transaction and what they need to understand.

Educated clients make better decisions.

Teaching does not mean that they understand HOW to do it. What's most important is that they understand what needs to be done and why.

If you can accomplish this within a story, it helps them better understand and cope with the situation during the transaction.

Be careful not to go overboard with teaching. It is an easy trap to fall into. If you teach them exactly how to do things, your audience will either be bored or they will feel like they do not need you anymore.

Focus on the big picture because that what most clients want to know and understand. There are too many variables in this business to fully answer a question to meet every circumstance.

Values

We want our customers to know that we are trustworthy. If we tell them, "We are Trustworthy!" Are they likely going to believe it?

NO!

They have to see an example. Or better yet a story that illustrates the value we want to share.

Think of parables and fables. These are ways to share your values and ideals with others in a way they can believe it.

Stories make values come to life in the eyes of your audience.

When you share your values, beliefs and passions, you will attract people who feel the same way. It helps to humanize and get to know you on a deeper level.

Most of us only share our values with our family and close friends. When we treat people like friends and family, they tend to do the same to us.

Validation

Validation comes from research. You should know their questions, concerns, worries, enemies, obstacles, values, desires and what angers them.

When you tell a story and a prospects says, "He knew what I was thinking," that is powerful. Unconsciously, they assume that you understand where they are coming from.

You start to be viewed as someone that they know and trust.

It's not like you are a mentalist or some kind of mind reader. You understand their concerns because you did the research to know who is your audience. And they will respect you for that.

This also gives you the opportunity to identify their objections first so you can start to break down their walls and connect on a personal level.

Validation helps us move from stranger to friend and from friend to expert in their eyes.

Benefits

A story (in my email system) does not have to follow the standard definition of a story. One way to do this would be to write about the benefits of working with you.

You could even do this in a list, which is a very popular type of content these days.

Benefits show people how you can help them solve their problems. This is important because that is the real reason they want to use a real estate agent.

The Essential Elements of a Compelling Story

If you want to hook your audience when they are reading your story, then you must incorporate these three elements of a compelling story: conflict, anticipation, and resolution.

Conflict represents the obstacles that the characters have to overcome in your story. Conflict builds tension, which makes the story interesting. Like the hardships that lead to the lessons learned. People want to know how others solved the same challenge and were successful. The tension created by conflict is what drives the story forward in the minds of your audience. Anticipation is the second element to a compelling story because it creates suspense. You don't want to tell every detail of the story because these facts are boring.

You want to leave a little to interpretation. They need to feel like something is going to happen, but they are not quite sure what it is. They can likely guess the outcome, but they do not know for sure.

Anticipation helps them to feel intelligent and that they are part of the story. This little bit of suspense helps them to participate in the story, if only in their minds.

It's the anticipation that makes you stick around until the end so you can see what really happens (even if you think that you already know).

Resolution is the third and last characteristic of a compelling story. Without resolution to the conflict, you leave the audience hanging at the end.

And there is nothing the audience hates more than conflict without resolution. It feels like betrayal.

The audience has invested time and emotion into your story and they feel cheated when they do not get to work it out. It's like getting into a fight with someone that you never see again. Without closure, the story can haunt us forever.

Stories by Theme

Whatever theme you choose at the beginning needs to be reflected in the story. Like I said earlier, the theme should run like a thread from the headline to the close. And possibly from one email to another.

This continuous theme encourages the buyer to keep on reading until the conclusion of the story. You've probably heard the old saying that humans are "creatures of habit."

This is because we follow familiar patterns through life and many times do not realize it.

When we see a familiar pattern, like a story theme, we will follow it until we are satisfied with the conclusion.

It's like the tease right before a television commercial. If we have an idea of what might be next, we are compelled to watch and see if it happens the way we expect.

An incomplete pattern is a puzzle that we are all dying to solve.

The themes we discussed in earlier chapters should also be used in your stories. Story Examples by Theme

The examples of stories by theme can be found in the appendix at the back of this book.

Tips and Tricks

- Talk to them, not at them. It's conversational.
- It's more about entertainment and less about data and information.
- Teaching what and why (not how to do it).
- Follow the Theme.
- Fully answer the questions raised in the headline and opening.
- Make them emotional.
- Pick a topic and start writing. Do it!

7
The Sell

"Don't forget to ask for the sale."

~ Robert Munzer - CEO, Entrepreneur, and my first mentor in sales

The influence in your writing comes from grabbing their attention with a great subject line, validating what they already

feel is important with a good story and then connecting their emotions to what you want them to do.

The sell contains two parts, the segue and the call to action. It's your opportunity to show what you can do for your prospects and then ask for the sale.

The Segue

When you get to this section while writing, go back and read the story again. But this time read it from the mind of your audience. You should have a pretty good idea how they would feel after reading your story because you did the research and asked the right questions.

You did do the research, right?

So, find a connection between that emotion and one of the following:

- A problem that you can help them solve
- A fear that they have where you can provide relief
- An obstacle that you can help them overcome
- An enemy that they do not see
- A benefit of working with you
- A need that you can meet
- A desire that you can fulfill

This is your opportunity to demonstrate how you can help your audience and solve their problems. Don't sell yourself short.

You can also think of a segue this way. It's simply a tool to transition between the story and the call to action. The segue primes the CTA in order to maximize the action taken.

Connecting a desire on an emotional level = Action.

One way to structure a segue is to pose a question. Try to anticipate a question that the audience might ask. Posing a question is a great device for leading someone to make the same conclusion and take action. If-Then statements are a great "low-key" way to ask a question and make a call to action in one sentence.

Here's a few different examples of a segue that I've used

- If you know someone who is heading in the wrong direction, then ...
- If you want a copy of the Cost Versus Value report, then ...
- What are you waiting for?
- What do you want to achieve?

Another great way to create a segue is by validating their feelings and then transitioning into what you want them to do.

Here are some examples of transitional phrases:

- I know it seems bad, but look at it this way... [When you are providing relief]
- If you think this is good, then wait until you... [When you are doubling down on benefits]

- While this may be true... [When you are trying to alter their perception]

The Call to Action [CTA]

More that 20 years ago, I helped solve a problem for a client and accidentally fell into sales.

I was working in Quality Assurance for a Medical Device Manufacturer. My job was to solve problems and make things more efficient.

And I understood our production capabilities better than anyone else in sales.

Which led me to work with clients on new products and help solve problems with existing ones.

My transition from operations to sales happened so fast and seamless that I didn't realize it myself.

As I was headed on my first sales call, my boss made sure that I knew the number one rule.

And I never forgot it.

"Don't forget to ask for the sale."

The call to action [CTA] is one of the final instructions that you will provide for your audience. This is your opportunity to ask for the sale or any action that you want your audience to take.

The power of the CTA is what drives people to take action. Good CTAs are typically built with a three part formula. Real estate is somewhat different than the traditional advertising model. Instead of selling physical products, you are selling services [relationships]. In order to use the three parts of the formula, you'll have to be creative. It's not a requirement to use all three parts with every CTA that you create.

Three Parts of a CTA

Part one of the CTA formula is the command.

For example, "Click on the link below."

You may have noticed that command sentences usually start with the action verb. This is ok, and there are other ways of structuring the command that are equally effective. This command is inspiring and harder to miss, "Don't wait another minute to put our team to work for you."

Part two of this formula is urgency.

Did you notice how I used it in the more creative example above?

"Don't wait another minute" is a less salesy way of creating a sense of urgency with your audience. That feeling that they just need to do it now.

Some writers will hype it up with the urgency, and it runs the risk of coming across negatively.

Some folks call the sense of urgency FOMO, or the Fear Of Missing Out. This fear is a powerful force because it taps into several layers of human emotions including: Panic, Greed, Comparison, Pride and Curiosity.

We are compulsively driven by fear so it is essential that it is built into your CTA.

Scarcity is another way to build urgency into your CTA. It tells the audience that if you don't do it now, you will not be able to do it later.

This is why companies have "limited time" offerings or the deal "ends tomorrow."

Hope can be used in place of fear as an effective tool for getting people to take action. With hope it is essential that your prospects understand that they have a problem, that the problem is big and that you have the best solution to the problem.

Part three of the formula is risk reduction.

Money back guarantees and free trial periods do not always cross over to Real Estate. You have to be more creative with your risk reduction statements.

There are two levels of risk in a real estate transaction. First, you have the obvious risks that everyone recognizes like a flaw in you as a real estate agent or in your business systems. Most people have developed ways to address these concerns.

For example, your first face to face with a client could be a "no obligation" appointment. They might be more inclined to meet with you if they know you are not going to beat them over the head with an agency agreement.

There are also hidden risks. These are different for each person, so you will have to dig deep with your clients to see what keeps them up at night.

One hidden risk might be that a buyer is concerned about defects that they might not be able to see. What can you offer that gives them relief from this pain?

One overlooked way to reduce risk is to be transparent.

For example, if you plan to send them a daily email, make sure that it is obvious in your CTA.

If you cannot come up with a way to remove risk, then another option is to showcase a benefit of working with you or wrap your CTA in a testimonial.

Showing them the value in taking the next step might be just what the doctor ordered.

Consistency in Action

You are not writing emails to make your prospects feel all warm and fuzzy. The purpose of your email is for them to take action.

When you leave out a call to action, you are wasting the goodwill generated with your readers. Some of them would have likely taken action if only they were nudged.

Don't feel that asking them to take action is detrimental to building a relationship. Never forget what we learned earlier, your goal is to get them to take the next step in the conversion process.

With your emails to prospects, the typical next step is to get in contact with you via email, phone or text. So that should be your typical call to action.

Never leave a call to action out of an email.

Never!

Ever!

Multiple CTAs

Most marketers will also tell you to have one and only one CTA in your email. Normally, I would agree with them.

If you are sending the email to prospects for nurturing, then you want to have another plan. The prospects in your database are in different places along the conversion pathway. Some are ready to move now and most want to move later.

So, in my nurturing email, I will have two CTAs. The first CTA is for the few who are ready now. My first call to action is usually a command for them to call me or reply to the email. My goal is to start a conversation and build a relationship with these people. If they have been on my list for a while, they will feel like they already know me, even though we have never met.

My second CTA is to the Daily Deal. This is one property that was recently listed in the MLS that is the best "value."

The second CTA will send them back to the listing on my search site. I've found that they will continue to look at other homes and pages once they get there. Sending them back creates a steady stream of recurring visitors and sets that habit of going to my site for real estate info.

I primarily use the second CTA for my "later" clients. Occasionally, a "now" client will want to see one of the Daily Deals. Guess who they call?

We will talk more about the second CTA in the next section, The Closing.

Examples of The Sell

Check out the appendix in the back of the book to see the different ways I used The Sell by theme. The appendix contains one complete email for each theme.

Tips and Tricks

- The best segue helps everything flow smoothly from the story to the call to action. Sometimes it's so smooth you don't realize what's happened. And that's what you want to achieve with your segue.
- The segue is your opportunity to show your value. Don't sell yourself short.
- Remember, your ultimate goal is to start a conversation and build a relationship.
- Keep a list of transitional phrases handy to pair with the emotions you are stirring.
- Tell them what you want them to do

- 1 (or at most 2) Calls to Actions Only
- Your CTA should be short. Either one or just a few sentences
- Create urgency. Remove risk
- A weak or non-existent CTA is a rookie mistake
- Avoid jargon or industry terms
- Seduction works better than pressure

8
The Closing

"I'm gonna make him an offer he can't refuse"

~ Don Vito Corleone, from the movie *The Godfather*

The closing and the sell should join forces to create an offer that your audience can't refuse. And not because they are under the threat of violence. Your offer should overwhelmingly show your audience the value and benefits of working with you over any other option.

Real estate is a long sales cycle. The average person starts investigating about one year before they plan to take action. Some start years in advance. Not everyone who signs up for your email is ready for a solution or even a conversation.

This is where the close comes into play for me. The first CTA is designed to capture those "Hot" Prospects who are ready (or almost ready) to take action. Like I said in the previous section, I typically use the close as a second CTA to build trust and a long term relationship with my audience.

Second CTA

My every weekday email is dubbed "The Daily Deal." In the close of every email, I use it as an opportunity to showcase the best "value" I could find in the homes that were listed in the past few days. Most of my audience considers themselves "value" shoppers (which is different from "price" shoppers) and so this section speaks directly to them and their desire to find a good deal.

Value shoppers are those who are interested in a good deal, and not so much the price. They like properties that have potential and have been overlooked by most other buyers and agents in the area. They are typically overlooked because of poor marketing (or less frequently over pricing).

For the Daily Deal, I provide a vague description of why they may be interested in this property and a link to the IDX listing on my website. I send them to the IDX listing page because their click meant they wanted more information on that specific property. The audience will quickly go away if there is a disconnect between what they were promised when they clicked and what they find on the landing page.

In addition to bringing more "value" to my audience, this results in additional traffic to my site from previous visitors. I find that they will typically visit five other pages while they are there. It also builds a habit of searching for homes and real estate information on my site. With an ever growing list of options, I'd prefer that they use my site where I can see their level of interest.

Other Options for the Close

If the daily deal is not your style, don't fear. There are other options that are equally effective in capturing the attention of those who are not ready to pull the trigger.

One option would be to show social proof in your close with a link to your reviews on another site. This doesn't build traffic to your site, but it can build trust. Typically, trust is built over time, which makes this a great opportunity to build that relationship each and every day.

Another opportunity would be to tease another benefit. Maybe a link to a related article that you previously wrote. If the audience was interested in this info, they might want to dig deeper in the same subject. Most of your audience will see this as a benefit. Having a library of trusted information on your site will put you ahead of 99.9% of other real estate professionals in your market.

The Footer Needs Love Too

I consider the email footer as part of the closing section. Make sure that you give that part some consideration.

One part of the footer that many forget is your contact info. I typically see two big problems with this section. Either it is lacking information or you have too much information. The footprint should be small because most people know to look at the bottom of the email

You do not need every way to contact you, but your phone number should be there. Most people can figure out your email address and website from the email that you sent. If you put every possible way to connect with you, then it looks spammy. Our goal is to not make the email look like spam. Our goal is to make the email look like it came from a friend.

If you are sending mass emails, make sure that you are following the federal and state laws for email and advertising. Make sure that you have a way to unsubscribe and to change preferences from your email footer.

Examples of Closing Themes
- Check out the appendix in the back of the book to see the different closings that I have used by theme. The appendix contains one complete email for each theme.

Tips and Tricks
- In our business NOT everyone is ready for a conversation, appointment or transaction.
- Tease another benefit

- Build trust
- Show social proof
- Provide your contact info
- Don't Look Spammy
- Close is consistent with the theme of the email
- Make sure there is a clear connection between the CTA and landing page.

9
How to Convert Online Leads

"Double down on your strengths and outsource the rest."

~ Steve Jolly

Writing the email is one part of the overall system to nurture and convert leads. You also need to promote the content that you created and spend time working your database to generate the leads. Focus on what you enjoy and what you do best, and then find others to do the rest of the work.

In this chapter, I want to share the systems and tools that I use in my email marketing system. This is not the only way to do it, however, it is the way that works best for me.

First, I want to talk about the tools that I use in this system and show you how they work for me.

Second, we will discuss the systems that I use to repurpose the content and prospect the people in my database.

Tools

In addition to a smartphone, I currently use four different tools in my marketing system: lead generating website, CRM, email marketing platform, and email account.

All of the tools that I use can serve more than one function in this list. However, that is not always the best. When you try to be everything to everyone, it is hard to keep up with the specific needs of your clients. Instead, I have found tools that work together in a complimentary way to achieve the results that I want. Feel free to use whatever works best for you.

Tracking

Before we dive into the tools, lets talk about one item that each of these tools should have. It is the ability to track activity. For example, you will want to know who is looking on your lead generating website and what they are looking at. And you will want to know who is opening your emails and clicking on your links. Tracking is not 100% foolproof. Some services block the ability to track and people will naturally look from other devices. So keep this in mind when reviewing data concerning your prospects. Just because tracking says they have not opened your email, don't take it to the bank.

Lead Generation Website

I am a strong proponent of SEO and that led me to buy my last website from Real Estate Webmasters (REW). Their sites are known for their strong SEO structure and a design that encourages conversion.

For this type of system, I strongly recommend something similar. The purpose of your website is to generate leads and see what those leads do while they are searching online. Most modern real estate website services will offer this information. I also decided to work with REW because their site integrates with my CRM, Follow Up Boss. So when I look at a prospect in my CRM, I can see virtually the same tracking info as when I look in the back end of my website.

Although REW has a robust CRM built into their backend, I also collect leads from other sources. So I need a CRM to capture all of that information in one place automatically.

Make sure that your site has a blog built in. This will be helpful to your prospects and enhance the visibility of your site.

If you do not have a site with IDX, you can also use a landing page to generate leads.

Email Marketing

I choose to use MailChimp as my email marketing tool because it is simple to use and syncs with my CRM and so many other programs.

I use MailChimp to send my every weekday email. It tracks the people who open and click on the emails that I send and then forwards that info (with the email) to Follow Up Boss.

So when I look at a prospect in Follow Up Boss, I can see all of the emails that they received, which ones they opened, how many times they opened the email and if they clicked on the email.

This info is valuable to you because it shows that someone is interested in what you have to say. It means they might be a step closer to taking action. We will talk more about these triggers, later in this chapter.

CRM

The CRM that I use is Follow Up Boss. I initially choose FUB because it works with 100's of lead sources, has a mobile app, syncs with my lead generating website, and syncs with my email marketing tool.

With Follow Up Boss, it is easy to create lists of people based on recent activity on your website or in your daily email. For example, I can create a list of people who opened and clicked on an email within the last seven days.

These lists are very flexible and powerful. You can create as many as you need, save them and combine actions from multiple sources of data.

Then you can easily scroll through the list of folks, see their recent actions and decide what is the best way to follow up.

These lists helps me decide who we should focus on and who we should leave alone. More to come on prospecting your database later in the chapter.

One last thing that I want to share about Follow Up Boss is the mobile app. The mobile app helps me to be authentic in the very first communication that I have with a lead. I don't use autoresponders to send that first email.

Autoresponders are easy to spot and they do not make a good first impression.

Instead, I use the template feature in the mobile app to send them a regular email (and text) from my iPhone as soon as the lead comes in. I know it is a small thing, however, I think it gives a better first impression and I get a better response.

G Suite (formerly Google Apps for Work)

The last tool that I use is a gmail account through G Suite. This account also syncs with the Follow Up Boss CRM. So when I send or receive a regular email to one of the people in my CRM, it is automatically pulled into Follow Up Boss.

This helps me keep track of all our recent conversations in one system that I use for prospecting. And any email sent by Follow Up Boss is sent through and also stored in my email. The way these two systems sync and work together is amazing.

Systems

Now that you know how to write and the tools that you need, then the next thing we need to cover is what to do with the emails you write.

Before we dive into the systems, I want to talk about their architecture. These systems were designed with the individual agent or small team in mind. They are simple enough that one person could do the work daily and effective enough to bring massive results.

Many people feel that it is impossible for the individual or small team to do content marketing effectively.

Today, I am going to show you a content marketing plan driven by email with proven results.

Theses are the systems that I am going to share with you:

1. **Five Star Prospects** - How to qualify leads in order to create clients
2. **Four Step Funnel** - How to guide your clients along the conversion path
3. **Five Star Emails** - How to start conversations that lead to sales

4. **Promotion Plan** - How to repurpose content to drive more sales

5 Star Prospects

In the chapter on Conversion Theory, we discussed 5 Star Prospects. *A 5 Star Prospect is someone who is:*

1. Willing to Communicate
2. Friendly and Cooperative
3. Know what they want
4. Knows when they want it
5. Wants us to help them

This information is helpful because it sets the bare minimum requirements in order for someone to work with you. If they have wrong or missing answers to any of these 5 Star questions, it's impossible to do business with them.

It is your job to find out the number of Stars for everyone in your database and help them get the next one. That makes it sound much harder than it really is.

Most of the people in your database will have zero stars and that's ok. You can't work with everyone because you do not have the time. This email-marketing program is a type of content marketing. It's designed to make people contact you first.

When they reply to one of your daily emails, that is a great opportunity to ask questions that help you decide if they can get to 5 stars.

If they consistently read your email, click on your links or search on your site. That is a trigger, almost like someone raising his or her hand. Use this opportunity to reach out, be helpful, and get additional questions answered.

In the section on 5 Star Emails, we will talk about the type of emails to send when triggered that can start conversations and help you get more qualifying answers.

First, we need to understand our database and how to move people through it.

Four-Step Funnel

The four-step funnel is one of the most effective ways you can turn prospects into clients. The effectiveness is built into the design. Part of it is the structure and the rest is due to the simplicity of the plan. It's easy enough for a single agent or a small team to do every week day.

1. Write and send a story based email every weekday to your list.
2. Respond quickly to those who reply.
3. Review database daily for triggers (People actively searching or opening)
4. Reach out to those people who trigger with one of the 5 star emails.

Everyone in your database is going to get your daily email. If someone reaches out to you, answer right away. If someone signals that they might be interested, show up and be helpful.

It's that simple.

And in reality, it is the same thing that we expect from other professionals when we are a potential customer.

We will talk more about those 5-star emails now.

5 Star Emails

5 star emails are simple emails that are designed to start conversations and answer the 5 Star qualifying questions.

In the beginning of this book, you learned how to write emails that inform and entertain your prospects so that they get to know, like and trust you.

With some people, this is all you need to get them to take action. With others, we may have to nudge them a little harder into taking that next step.

That's where the 5 Star emails come into play.

These emails work best when you send them to clients who are active on your site or reading your emails but have not yet responded. They are the dollars hidden in your database.

Most real estate professionals will ignore these prospects because they do not know how to work their database to get results. They don't understand how to start real estate conversations with people online or by email.

And that's what most of us want from our leads...an opportunity for a real estate conversation with someone that is interested in buying or selling a home.

Here's how I suggest you use them

You should be sending consistent emails to your clients with tracking.

Review your database regularly for triggers - those who are actively opening emails, clicking on links, or searching homes on your website.

Reach out to each of these people with one of the 5 Star emails, text or phone call. It doesn't matter how you reach out, only that you do it.

I would limit it to one of these 5 Star email per week (in addition to the weekday email) until they respond.

When they reply, keep the conversations rolling by answering their concerns and then following up with a question.

Remember, our goal is to find the 5 Star prospects.

These questions should be about what type of home that they want to buy, what concerns they have about selling their home and the time frame to complete the transaction.

Each question and response should get us closer to finding out if they have 5 Star potential or not. I call the emails used to start conversations and ask questions, the 5 Star Emails.

Here are some examples of 5 Star Emails

1. Subject: Coffee?

I have a few hours available later this week, if you want to see a few homes or talk about real estate.

What does your schedule look like?
Talk soon,
[Your Signature]

2. Subject: Your thoughts?
When did you want to [buy a/sell your] home?
Take care,
[Your Signature]

3. Subject: I need to apologize
I meant to ask what you "must have" in your next home?
Any deal killers?
Take care,
[Your Signature]

4. Subject: Your Home Search
Are you still looking to [buy a/sell your] home?
Thank you,
[Your Signature]

5. Subject: Quick Question
What can I do to earn your business?
Sincerely,
[Your Signature]

How to write your own 5 Star Emails

5 Star emails are short, personal emails that ask a question in order to start (or continue) a conversation with a prospect.

The question in the email can qualify one of the 5 Stars or it could be based on a concern that they should have at their location on the conversion pathway.

The question can be something they are thinking about or something that they should be concerned with at this point in the process.

It's really that simple.

5 Star Email Q&A

What if they don't respond?
That's ok. Keep sending them the regular weekday email. Occasionally, send one of the 5 Star Emails in this report if they are actively reading your emails or searching on your website.

What if they are not friendly and cooperative?
If you still want to work with them, prepare for the headache. Remember that you don't have to put up with nonsense and life is too short to work with miserable people. Unless there is some compelling reason, I don't have a lot of tolerance for people who continuously choose to act this way.

What if they don't know what they want?
That's ok. Spend some time helping the prospect discover what works best for them and where they want to live. Reasonable people should be able to decide when given enough information. This could be a good prospect who needs some guidance.

What if they don't want to move now?

That's ok. Find out where they stand on the other stars and stay in touch with them. Occasionally, ask where they stand on their timeline or send them one of the 5 Star Emails. This may be a good prospect for the future if you stay in touch and demonstrate the value in working with you.

What if they don't want us to help them?

We have two choices here. Either, work on demonstrating your value in hopes of convincing them or decide to move on and fish in better waters. Sometimes it's best to move on because we want to focus our time on those who are most likely to be 5 Star Prospects and not worry about the rest.

As soon as people know what they want and when they want it, I move them to Hot Prospect status in my CRM and another level of marketing.

How to add automation to this system

Follow Up Boss helps me add automation to this system with their lists and email templates. I've loaded a bunch of these 5 Star emails into Follow Up Boss and made them templates. This means that I can scroll through the list of people who triggered, easily review our past communications and send a 5 Star email with just a few clicks.

And then click to the next person in the list and repeat.

It makes this process very fast considering these are individual emails and not coming from an auto-responder.

Make sure you set aside time in the few hours following this exercise to respond to those who replied. Keep the conversations rolling and solve their problems. This is how you start to develop relationships with your online prospects that lead to sales.

Promotion Plan

In order to get the most out of the content you create, I recommend having a plan to promote your content on other marketing channels besides email. This plan helps you to re-purpose your content and drive people to take action.

Re-purposing content is the icing on the cake. It is one of the best ways to maximize the effectiveness from the email pieces that you create. The Promotion Plan will be the core principle of promoting our content online. However, it would be unwise to share it exactly the same way across all of the different channels. You will have to slightly adjust your content on each channel so that it appears to be within the standard context for the platform you use.

In other words, how you tell a story on Facebook is different than the way it is told on Instagram. Take that into account as you promote your work.

1. Create an image for your email that helps tell the story. You will not send this image in your email, but will use it in other areas of your content promotion. You can watermark the image with your website URL. Use a descriptive name in both the file name and title tag of the image. I currently use the apps WordSwag and Typorama on my phone to create images. These tools provides a nice selection of royalty free images

with an amazing text editor. It makes telling a story through short text and images very easy.

2. Post your email on your blog and include the image in the blog post. You might need to correct any references to email or any CTAs like "hit reply. I usually change the words "email" to "post" and "hit reply" to "comment below."

3. Share this blog post on your Facebook business page. The image should pull automatically into the post. If you do not have a Facebook business page, you can share it on your personal page but do it sparingly. Your personal page should be more personal than business. If someone engages your page, reply quickly. At a minimum, you should mirror any engagement that your receive. If you receive a like, then like back. If you receive a short comment, reply with a similar comment. To speed up your results, you should attempt to create relationships with those who engage you and those who you think would be good clients, referral partners and friends.

4. Pin the image in the blog post to Pinterest. This can be completed in a few clicks if you add the Pinterest "Pin It" button to your browser. If you pin it from your blog post, it will automatically pull in the link to your post and the blog post title in the text preview. I usually put my opening in this text section instead of the title.

5. Post the image on Instagram and connect to your blog post I create all of my images on my phone, so it is easy to post on Instagram. Open Instagram and use

the image in your camera roll. Add filters or any other desired effects, if you want. Tell a short story, compelling story in the caption section. Add 10 – 20 relevant hash tags that go with the theme of your post and image in the first comment. Some of these hashtags should have very high post counts (100,000 –1,000,000+). This will give you some immediate engagement from the high number of people searching these popular hashtags. Some of these hashtags should have an medium amount of post counts (10,000 – 100,000) because these hash tags will give you engagement over a longer period of time. Since these tags are used less often, your post stay higher on the list. If someone engages your post, reply quickly. At a minimum, you should mirror any engagement that your receive. If you receive a like, then like back. If you receive a short comment, reply with a similar comment. To speed up your results, you should attempt to create relationships with those who engage you and those who you think would be good clients, referral partners and friends.

It is important to respond quickly to any engagement that you receive from your content marketing. This will keep your audience happy, encourage more conversations and further develops your relationship. So it is important to have time to respond in the immediate hour after you promote your content. It is ok to do other things during this time. However, we need to be ready to respond quickly.

This plan is just the bare minimum that I recommend for your content marketing strategy. You could easily add other channels, drive paid traffic at your blog post or remarket to past visitors. Use forms to capture the contact info for any new readers of your blog content, especially if you are sending paid traffic to your blog posts.

The promotion side of your content marketing likely takes 15 - 30 minutes for each email that you write. After you systemize it, you can pass it on to an assistant or intern who is working for you.

The creation side of your marketing takes shouldn't take any longer than 23 minutes. It might take longer at first, but you will get faster and write better over time.

10
Real Email Examples

Below you will find an example of an email that I wrote and sent for each one of the ten themes listed earlier in this book. This is not a comprehensive list of possible themes, but consider it a good set of tools for your email toolbox.

These emails are meant for your inspiration only. Even if you copied them word for word, they would not work for your audience or your personality. So, be inspired without ripping off someone else's work word for word.

Inspirational

How one simple act can create something amazing

In 1865, Columbus, Mississippi was a small railroad town of 6,000 people due south of Shiloh, Tennessee. Due to their proximity to the rail line and the war, they became known as a hospital town.

In the two-day battle at Shiloh, there were more than 3,500 soldiers killed and 16,000 wounded on both sides.

Nearly every home and business in Columbus was used as a hospital.

4 Generals, 2,500 Confederate soldiers and 32 Union soldiers were buried in Friendship Cemetery during the war.

And when the war was over, something amazing happened.

On April 25th, 1866, four ladies who lived in Columbus gathered to decorate the graves of the Confederate soldiers with flowers. While there, they felt compelled to honor the Union soldiers and share in their family's grief. So, they decorated their graves with flowers too.

Their story of love and forgiveness spread throughout Mississippi. A reporter for the *New York Tribune* took that story north and published it.

Francis Miles Finch, a Yale graduate and Judge, read the story and was moved to write the poem, "The Blue and Gray."

"The Blue and Gray" was published in *The Atlantic* magazine in 1867 and the rest is history.

It's amazing how one simple act of love can culminate in the holiday known as Memorial Day.

So now you know it's as much about reconciliation as remembrance.

The last two lines of the poem read: Love and tears for the Blue, Tears and love for the Gray.

Take some time this weekend to love and remember, remember and love.

See you on Tuesday!

The Daily Deal in Nashville is ...

Origin Stories
Why I never wear green on St. Patricks Day

For most people, St. Patrick's Day is a celebration of all things Irish. For me, it is a celebration of my dad and his influence on my life.

He would have been 77 years old today and still smiling.

There are so many things he taught me, and I probably don't remember them all. The one that stuck with me the most was his belief in me.

He often said this to me, "You can do anything that you want to do in life, if only you set your mind to it."

I'm not sure why this one stuck, but I'm glad that it did. It has certainly served me well over the years.

Like when my heart was set on going to the Air Force Academy, and he helped me get a nomination from our Congressman, Al Gore Jr.

Or, in my first "real" job out of college in the medical device industry. I had a huge project to get a new international certification for our company called ISO 9001. At the time, consultants and colleagues were telling us that it couldn't be done without help and at a cost of +$200,000. Instead, we did it in-house in half the time and at 10% of the expected cost.

Or, when I wanted to be a professional fundraiser for the American Heart Association in his honor. We had double-digit increases two years in a row (during a recession) and raised over $1,000,000 in a mostly rural area of Middle Tennessee.

Or, when I decided to become a Realtor and sell bank-owned properties. I was told that it was nearly impossible to break into the business, and it would take more than two years to get my first listing. I listed and sold thirteen bank-owned homes in my first full year in 2006. That was well before the market crashed.

I learned from him not to listen to the naysayers and those who said it couldn't be done. I learned that most things were not impossible. They were just harder than most people were willing to work.

So if you are facing an impossible task today, I know exactly where you are coming from.

I'd love to talk to you about those obstacles that are standing in your way. And help you find a path from where you are today, to where you want to be.

The Daily Deal in Nashville is…

Shocking

The Bizarre Antics of House Hunting TV

It was a great day. One of my clients closed on his Tennessee home today.

He is an aspiring singer/songwriter with much talent, youthful energy, and the drive to make it happen.

A few months ago, during the search process, he discovered that one of the National House Hunting TV shows was looking for someone moving to Music City for one of their upcoming episodes. He thought this would be a great way to introduce himself (and his talent) to his new hometown. He applied to be on the show and was selected in the first round.

As he was telling me the story, I was excited for him.

Then he asked me if I would agree to be on the show. My first thought was, "I bet I could talk Gretchen (my fabulous Wife and Realtor) into doing the show."

But that wouldn't be right.

So, I looked at him and said, "If you want to be on the show, I will do it for you."

We got busy finding a home to buy, completing the inspections, and getting ready for the closing. But, I soon forgot about the TV show.

On the way to the closing today, my client reminded me about the show and told me he decided against it.

He stated that the filming took several weeks, and they wanted you to already have a home under contract.

Then they would film you for about a week, looking at three other homes for sale, even though you have another one under contract in real life.

Once you closed on your house, then they would then film you like you were looking at your house for the first time.

And you could not move in yet.

Finally, a few more weeks after closing the show would film one last time like you just moved into the home.

Does this sound crazy to you too?

Like a semi-truck stuck in reverse, that's a whole lot of backwards.

So the next time you see one of those shows, where they look at three homes and buy in less than thirty minutes, remember this.

Things aren't always as they seem in real estate, especially on TV.

In the meantime, if you want the Real Story on real estate in Nashville, just hit reply.

This Deal of the Day in Nashville is…

Demonstation

The Secret to Our Success

22 years ago, I made the best decision of my life. (Happy Anniversary, Gretchen!)

Just like everyone else, the path was not always easy for us.

There were twists and turns. Bumps in the road and streams to cross.

We occasionally took a wrong turn and had to find our way back home.

There were also moments along the way that made everything worthwhile.

Many days full of laughter and hope, spent together and with friends and family.

We didn't always know what we were doing.

However…

We were committed; we held each other's hand, said I'm sorry, offered forgiveness and never gave up.

We never stayed mad for long; we said I love you, did our best, worked hard, and never gave up.

This is the secret to our success (and happiness).

Why we love working together in real estate.

The reason we are still together after 22 years.

We never gave up on our relationship.

We never gave up on each other.

We never gave up on love.

We never gave up.

In the spirit of Love, we want to say thank you to all of our wonderful friends and clients.

This Deal of the Day in Nashville is…

Pop Culture
One man's trash is another man's $500,000

Stan Caffy was a local pipefitter who liked to look for odd and old things, especially at garage sales. In the mid-nineties, he found an old, stained parchment of the Declaration of Independence and paid $2 for it. He purchased it to hang in his Donelson garage where Stan liked to work on bikes.

Nine years later Stan Caffy married Linda. Linda thought Stan was a packrat who collected things and put them in the garage. Linda pushed him to clean the garage while they were combining households. After a year, they decided to donate the parchment and several other items to the local thrift store.

Linda took the Declaration, an antique table, a showerhead and faucet to the thrift store in Nashville. When she took it, she told the thrift shop that it might be worth something and they should check it out.

Almost one year later, Michael Sparks was scouring through the Music City Thrift Store and spotted the Declaration of Independence. He paid $2.48 for the copy and brought it home.

He knew there was something special about this document.

Michael, a music equipment technician, did some homework in his spare time.

He soon discovered that the parchment turned out to be an "official copy" of the Declaration of Independence. It was one of two hundred copies commissioned by John Quincy Adams when he was Secretary of State in 1820.

He thought they might be able to get $100,000 for the document and put it up for auction a month later with Raynors' Historical Collectible Auctions in Burlington, NC. Six bidders contended for the document and the winning bid was $477,650.

(After taxes) Michael had a small fortune and a great story to tell.

Like Michael, we scour the market for value and act quickly to take advantage of every opportunity. If this sounds good, hit reply to discuss a winning strategy customized for you.

This Deal of the Day in Nashville is …

Current Events
Hot chicken on a Brexit

I've held off on writing about the Brexit until the dust settled and calmer heads prevailed.

The stock dumping tsunami subsided on Tuesday when bargain hunters flooded the exchanges to scoop up deals. And we are seeing the same thing happening today.

Like most, you are probably wondering how this change in European politics will affect the Nashville market.

The long-term outlook is unclear. It depends on the ability of these politicians to set aside their petty grievances and separate in orderly fashion. If that happens, I do not expect any significant changes for Nashville.

For the short term, this is what I expect for Nashville.

For the last ten years, the stock market has been full of uncertainty. In times of crisis, money flows to safer havens to avoid unnecessary risk.

That means I expect more international investment in the most secure country on earth, the United States of America.

While people will continue to invest their money in the stock market, I expect they will be hedging their bets by investing in real estate.

Although, real estate has taken its share of lumps over the last decade, it is still seen as a safer bet than the stock market by many financial experts.

Since Nashville is known internationally and is getting lots of accolades, I expect we will have more investment from outside of Tennessee in our wonderful city.

This movement will likely continue to push up prices for residential and commercial real estate.

This is great news for homeowners and not so great news for those looking to buy a home in Nashville.

However, there is a silver lining in this disaster for home buyers. The uncertainty in the market is expected to hold interest rates lower at a time when the Federal Reserve was moving in the opposite direction. Some experts expect the rates to dip below the 3.33% average for 30-year mortgages in 2012, which was our all time low.

We've never experienced a market quite like the one we've enjoyed for the last few years. When a market is appreciating, you would expect that the mortgage rates would be climbing with it.

This is not the case. Low rates with an improving market make it a great opportunity for both buyers and sellers. I'm not sure we will see this again in our lifetimes.

If you've been considering making a move and are not quite sure about the market, let me know what you are thinking.

I'd love to hear from you!

The Daily Deal in Nashville is...

[FYI - Nashville is synonymous with Hot Chicken and Biscuits hence the word-play subject line for this email]

Conflicting Information
A falling appraisal in a rising market

My clients and friends know they can ask me questions about Real Estate any time; I am always happy to help.

Most of the time people ask me before they take action. I like that best because it gives me the most opportunity to help someone. Every now and then, someone asks after the fact.

In these cases, sometimes we can help, and sometimes it is too late.

When in doubt, just ask. Don't think you are bothering me.

Here's a good question I ran across the other day from a homeowner (not a client). They bought a house early in 2015 in a rush and did not get the best mortgage to meet their needs. They decided to refinance in the New Year and started the process.

They did not have a strategy or a plan and once again trusted in the process. When their refinance appraisal came back, the value was 3% less than they paid a few months earlier. In addition, the new loan required PMI (Private Mortgage Insurance) for 4 years due to the appraisal even though they put 20% down initially.

Needless to say, the refi fell through. They felt cheated out of their time and the $450 for the appraisal.

They wanted to know if they should file a formal complaint.

I explained that it is easier to do it right the first time than to go back and try to fix this mess. When we sell a home, we put together a packet of information about the home and recent comps for the appraiser. Sometimes it is 30+ pages long. We also provide a tour of the home and answer any questions the appraiser has immediately. It helps to build a case for the value of the property. We can't set the value, but we can provide honest data and information that supports our claim.

For the best success, I recommend that you do this same process when you refinance your home.

Let me know your questions about the real estate market or your Nashville home in the comments below.

The Deal of the Day in Nashville is...

Taking a Stand
Buyers are liars, even in Mayberry

Despite all of his shortcomings, Barney Fife is one of the most lovable characters in Mayberry. In one episode, Barney decides that being a real estate agent is going to be his new career and starts to line up a chain of sales including the home of Andy Griffith.

While all of this is happening, Opie is trying to sell his bike to a friend without disclosing all of the defects. Andy happens upon the transaction and stops it in its tracks when he tells the truth about the bike.

Andy tells Opie, "When you are selling something, the buyer has a right to know everything that's wrong with it, otherwise it's not quite honest."

Later in the show, Barney brings his clients to Andy's home for a showing. Barney does his best to showcase the home, and Opie does his best to make sure that the buyer's know everything wrong about the home. And I mean everything. It's not long until the buyers are running out the door.

When they leave everyone is mad at Opie because they thought he was getting revenge for losing the bike sale. Then, Opie reminds Andy of what he said earlier about honesty.

That funny episode shows how people change when money is involved. You can watch it here: [Link to episode on Youtube]

In my experience, I've found that most people are honest in their real estate transactions. Every so often you run across that bad apple. They give buyers, sellers, and Realtors a bad name and a tough obstacle to overcome.

I'm usually good at discerning people's intentions, but the best manipulators have a unique ability to fly under the radar.

These hucksters might think they are getting away with something, but they usually get caught in the process. And in the end, they have wasted much of your time and energy.

It would be easy to get cynical about real estate over time. I decided to go in another direction. Instead of blindly trusting everyone, I will trust first and then verify.

By verify, I mean dig deep. If you receive a pre-approval letter from a buyer that's a great start. If you have any concerns about getting to the closing table, pick up the phone and talk to the lender. Explain your concerns and ask them to provide a reasonable answer. If they don't give you the answer you need, ask more questions.

Hold them accountable for the reporting requirements in the contract. Follow up to make sure they are upholding their end of the bargain. These things do not guarantee that it will close, but they sure put the odds in your favor.

What's your single, biggest concern with real estate transactions?

The Deal of the Day in Nashville is…

Social Proof

Three rules of highly effective organizations as developed by the Special Forces

Yesterday, I told you about Tennessee State Senator Mark Green.

He came to speak at a Leadership GNAR (Greater Nashville Association of Realtors) meeting about leading highly effective organizations, and all I told you about was his interview with Saddam Hussein the night he was captured in Iraq.

That story about the interview was so fascinating that I had to share it first.

And, that's NOT all that I have to say about that...

Senator Green has a long career full of amazing accomplishments. Here is a list of a few of them:

Graduated from West Point with a degree in economics

Masters in Information Systems from the University of Southern California

Doctor of Medicine as an Emergency Room Surgeon

Ranger in the 82nd Airborne Division

Flight Surgeon for Special Operations Aviation Regiment

Founder/CEO of Align MD – Emergency Room Staffing Company serving 34 hospitals

So to say that Senator Green has experience with highly effective organizations would be an understatement.

He talked about many aspects of leadership and this one thing caught my attention.

Senator Green said that these are "Three Keys to a Highly Effective Organization":

- Trust
- Tough Love
- Buy-In

And I agree with him. It's impossible for a group of people to work together without trust. How much money does the American Automotive Industry loose every year because many people still do not trust the quality of American-made cars. And their quality is better than ever. It's so hard to get back trust once it's lost.

Setting high expectations and pushing hard to achieve them is this version of Tough Love. The Navy Seals discovered long ago that when you are ready to quit, you still have more than half a tank left. Many people are attracted to and thrive in high achieving environments.

It would be hard to argue with buy-in. It's hard to work together effectively if everyone is running a different playbook. Senator Green suggested one of the best ways to get buy-in from your team is to love on them. Do what you can to love on your people and they will love you to the moon and back.

This also reminds me of family.

And if you are looking for a broker who will treat you like family, then let's sit on the porch and talk about it.

The Daily Deal in Nashville is...

Answering Questions
What's your home really worth?

One of the first things you do when you are thinking about selling your home is to determine its value.

The "true" value is determined by what a ready, willing and able buyer will pay for your home.

But, we want to know the value before we put it on the market.

Since every home and lot is different, this task is more art than science.

So, let's look at the typical ways people attempt to determine value and see downside of each approach.

One of the first places people look is the appraised value computed for property taxes. This is typically the least accurate of all the approaches. These values are usually based on property data and rarely on a personal visit to the neighborhood, let alone the inside of your home. It has nothing to do with the value of your home and everything to do with the taxes you will pay.

Picture someone in a cubicle throwing darts at numbers on the wall. This is a tax appraisal.

The second common approach is a tool like the Zestimate from Zillow. The industry name for this type of estimate is an Automated Valuation Model or AVM.

The AVM is a step above the tax appraisal and still not perfect. They use a set of data similar to the tax appraisal and they apply mathematic modeling to calculate the value at a certain point in time.

This is a better approach, however, it still does not factor in the individuality of your home. The model does not see that you upgraded the kitchen and master bath last year. This type of evaluation is more accurate for cookie cutter homes in large neighborhoods and less accurate for everyone else.

Appraisers and experienced real estate agents offer the best opportunity to get an accurate number. However, in determining value they are always looking backwards. They look for current listings and recent sales in your area. If your market is rapidly appreciating (like Nashville), the value six months ago could be significantly less than the value today.

Since these professionals will likely be coming inside your home, also make sure they are aware of everything that you have done to improve the home. Don't be afraid to show lists of improvements, invoices, before/after photos and anything else you can do to document the work completed.

Be sure to ask how they are make adjustments for time and improvements, and check their work afterwards.

Who wants to leave money on the table?

If you are thinking about selling your home and want to know the value, then hit reply and I'd be glad to talk to you about it.

The Daily Deal in Nashville is...

Made in the USA
Lexington, KY
17 October 2018